Eight Things You Need to Know to Write a Novel

Eight Things You Need to Know to Write a Novel

by

Jan Holmes Frost

Fireship Press
www.FireshipPress.com

ISBN-13: 978-1-61179-132-7

BISAC Subject Headings:

LAN005000	LANGUAGE ARTS & DISCIPLINES / Composition & Creative Writing
REF026000	REFERENCE / Writing Skills
LAN014000	LANGUAGE ARTS & DISCIPLINES / Reference

Address all correspondence to:
Fireship Press, LLC
P.O. Box 68412
Tucson, AZ 85737
Or visit our website at:
www.FireshipPress.com

2.0

Foreword

Why does a writer get hooked on writing and creating characters that arrive on the scene juggling baggage, drama and conflict?

Because we can!

It's our obligation to observe and record these stories and offer them in sacrifice to be devoured by a world filled with eager readers.

We write for those who want to delve into the life of a character and share the inherent crises and changes that must come, and to place themselves into a new and intriguing role. We write to offer escape into an alternate world filled with terror, sorrow, exhilaration, or love. But most of all, we write to leave an impact on the reader's life.

When I lived in an area that had little to offer in the way of networking among writers, I assembled materials collected during my novice years—college, workshops, seminars, and conferences—and started a series of writer's groups and workshops.

Experience had taught me that a busy author needs a compact, well-organized desktop companion, and what you will find in this book is the end (and tested) product.

Do you have shelves filled with 'How To' books on writing? Do you want a compact, concise, well-organized compilation that offers practical exercises? This book is an attempt to meet all of these needs.

Many well-known authors tell of the muse who keeps them up until three in the morning commanding them to produce inspired pages. The following day, when these same authors review what was written during the fray, they wonder if someone else was working on their computer—the writing is of such high quality.

This is part of the heady magic of being a writer! If you have yet to experience this, look out, because you're in for an epiphany!

Having said this, I nevertheless recommend Anne Lamott's *Bird by Bird* and Stephen King's *On Writing*, for inspiration and honest, succinct lessons. Also add to your library *The Chicago Manual of Style* and *Thanks, But This Isn't For Us*, by Editor, Jessica Page Morrell. (She tells it like it is from the publishing world of rejections). Yes, we can hone our craft—No, not everyone has the innate ability to produce good fiction.

Contents

ONE:
Things You Need To Know About Concept

New Beginnings

Each morning, with our first cup of coffee in hand, we formulate our plans for the day. This is true of homemakers, mothers, fathers, some students, businessmen and multi-millionaires. My hunch is that many world leaders make plans over their morning Joe.

This is in the real world. But your muse is other-worldly and he (she or it) will wake you in the middle of the night, slap a brilliant concept into your groggy brain and when you can't remember it the next day, he'll pout you both into a creative stupor.

Does a literary muse exist? Ask many famous authors including Stephen King who claims to have an evil, demanding elf residing in a hole beneath his desk. Other writers love to share stories of a muse who whispers in their ear. Muses represent the essence of our creative subconscious. They are ruthless, driving, honest, forthright, and they refuse to be ignored.

But if, for the moment, you'd rather not place your writing career in the hands of a mythical being, and you choose to ignore (at your own risk) the voice of that mystical inner voice, you're probably asking yourself a more practical question like:

What do I *really* know about the craft of writing *a novel?*

To be an avid reader does not a novelist make.

Whether you excelled in school writing courses or not, there are nevertheless fundamentals that have been forgotten, overlooked, or you just didn't get in the first place. As with any profession, there is a common structure, or skeleton, if you will, made up of basics. We may think we know these things about creating a work of fiction, but veteran authors will beg to differ. We must, and there are few exceptions, pay our dues in diligence.

Now that you are prepared to commit to the muse, the next question arises: Where do I begin?

Remember, nothing written - nothing read

What Will You Write?

"I could write a book."

These words are the herald's cry of an experience that begs to be memorialized in the form of a short story, memoir or novel.

"I have an idea, but where do I begin?"

You're stuck on where to get started. It could mean you're looking for structure and formatting.

"Where and how do great writers come up with their ideas?"

Some of us have vivid theatrical productions currently playing in the movie houses of our minds, but putting these on paper can be intimidating.

We each have life experiences, family sagas and stories passed down from our ancestors that would win literary achievement awards, if we could but properly capture them.

> *"Writing is easy; all you do is sit, staring at a blank sheet of paper (computer screen) until the drops of blood form on your forehead."*
>
> *Gene Fowler*

Themes and Premises

According to Henry James, one writer discovered his concept when he walked by the window of a seminary and caught a glimpse of a dinner party. A mere glimpse! Look at the millions of these little 'glimpses' we have available to us every day.

Rob the Cradle – Many famous writers, such as Tolstoy, Dickens and Mark Twain, have borrowed from their childhood.

Rob the Grave – Our ancestors have stories they've passed down through generations. If one of these thrillers grabs your attention, go ask Grandma—she may have the facts you need.

Draw on Life Experiences – During our lifetime we encounter situations that can be shared, elaborated on and fictionalized.

Beg, Borrow or Steal from everyday life – Often you can generate a basic theme for your book by just paying attention to the things you learn in the world around you.

For example, *Listening to the Corn Grow,* (a women's saga) evolved from a true and heart-wrenching tale told in maybe ten sentences about two women and their families living in a farming community in Central California during the nineteen-forties.

Ten years later, while driving along a remote stretch of highway, I topped a hill and was greeted by fields of corn..Mid-summer bright green stalks with golden tassels reaching heights of six feet or more faded into the distance.

The words came to mind, (perhaps directed by my muse), *"...listening to the corn grow."* I recalled this cliché that originated in the heartland of our country, *"It was so quiet you could hear the corn grow."* My muse took this and ran with it. Characters came to life amidst the corn fields of Nebraska and developed into a sweeping 120,000 word family saga—from a tiny glimpse of a real-life situation.

Mix fact with fiction – Factual places, authentic historical records, local news and stories can be crafted into a best-selling novel by adding the key ingredient, your imagination. We see themes like love won—or love lost—and good triumphs over evil, repeated time and again. What you need to do is imagine, research, and create an interesting new variation on one of these themes.

Think about how you conduct a journey. You don't aimlessly wander down highways hoping to arrive in midtown Manhattan. Even with modern GPS technology, you must still plan your route. Likewise with creating a work of fiction.

There is no such thing as an idea that is used up. Add a new slant, change things up a bit, and make it your own.

> *"There's nothing to writing. All you do is sit down at a typewriter and open a vein."*
>
> *Red Smith*

A Few Ever-Present Themes:

Love, Hate, Birth, Death, Murder, Betrayal, Fantasy, Reality.

Why do you see these themes so often? Because they are timeless and people find each of them fascinating.

Concept Development

Take this short quiz to examine the merits of your concept:

1. Does my concept contain elements that readers will identify with? What are they?

2. Do I have a concise through-line (aka story line or elevator pitch—what you say when someone asks about your book) that can be stated in one or two sentences? (Write it down and keep it in front of you, reworking it as changes occur.)

3. Does my concept pose challenges and obstacles for my protagonist to overcome? How?

4. Will the tension between my characters, or created by the obstacles they deal with, hold the reader's interest? You must add new problems with every twist and turn. How?

5. Does my concept define my characters in unique and fascinating ways? How?

6. What genre does this concept fit with?

7. What era, location, setting, time period is involved?

8. What other work would I compare this with?

9. How familiar am I with this concept?

10. Who is my target audience?

Write What You Know?

Creative writing instructors love to expound on this notion. A different opinion was voiced by a best-selling author during an interview. The essence of his argument was:

If we stick with writing what we know, then what becomes of imagination?

To be sure, it's tricky to describe the scent of a rose if you're dicing an onion. As a rule of thumb, write what you know, especially if you're an expert on a subject; but mix this up with your imagination. (Your muse?) Either that or take up writing ***non***fiction!

> *"When I stepped from hard manual work to writing, I just stepped from one kind of hard work to another.*
>
> *Sean O'Casey*

Premise – Plot – Resolution

Is the concept for your fiction beating on your subconscious mind, yelling to be set free? Is your muse whispering in your ear? If so, then now is the time for you to take things from *Premise,* to *Plot,* to *Resolution.*

When it's a concept (i.e. a **premise**), your story is like an unborn child. Once it's born, you will see how he or she grows, and record what happens (i.e. the **plot**). But raising a child demands structure, as does your story. When your child becomes a young adult and is ready to leave home, the cycle is complete (i.e. the **resolution**).

The point here is that every step of the way these three things – your ***premise-plot-resolution***, need nurturing, common sense, education, love and a great imagination.

As with a child, plan ahead for who your characters will become and what they will achieve; but don't be surprised if ultimately they switch things up and decide to follow a different path.

Writing Style

What is Your Writing Style?

To discover our personal writing style, we must first strip away the do's and don'ts and focus on raw, gut-level creative imagination. With writing, as with any craft, we need to learn, practice, and hone our skills. But there is no arguing that one source exists for artistic talent—YOU. You have a unique style, and as you begin to write fiction, this will emerge, and set you apart from everyone else.

Does our style change as we get into our character's head?

Yes! This can be compared to experiencing multiple personalities. Think about your own life. We change our style —how we think, dress, talk, and appear several times during a day.

YOU in the morning when you crawl out of bed = Raw style. You look in the mirror and there you are—the basics—a face that hasn't been re-designed by the razor, or made-up with layers of cosmetics.

YOU the grade school teacher = Teacher Role. To get from bed to the classroom takes minimal change, but you'll display a fresh clean face, smiles, gritting of the teeth, and occasionally a firm demeanor and tone of voice. You've taken on personal professional characteristics and changed your basic style.

YOU on a hot date = Romantic Role. Does this role reveal the true you, or do you act out who you think you should be for the occasion? Will you play the part of a seductress, or a casual charmer? This is where you dress the part and do whatever it takes to look your best—including spray-on body tans, pricey clothing, and credit card debt.

Somewhere beneath this gorgeous, sexy masquerade is the raw you that tumbled out of bed this morning. Did you think it would be any different for your characters?

Think of these contrasts as a kaleidoscope of the mind projected onto the written page.

A writer owns an inner voice and style. You project this according to who your characters are. Do we live our lives vicariously through our characters? Absolutely. It is part of the fun in creating and crafting fiction.

> *"The books one reads in childhood, and perhaps most of all the bad and good bad books, create in one's mind a sort of false map of the world, a series of fabulous countries into which one can retreat at odd moments throughout the rest of life, and which in some cases can even survive a visit to the real countries which they are supposed to represent."*
>
> George Orwell

Technique, Style, and Voice

Our combined technique and style is often labeled *Voice.* Don't look for it, it will find you from the recesses of your being. We'll cover voice, dialogue and point of view further in a later lesson. Voice cannot be taught or learned, but it can be developed and defined.

Are we who we read?

From childhood fiction to the classics, our memory retains the words we feed it. This is not to say that if we read the 'Bard', we'll pen Shakespearean quality prose. But the books we graze on can have an affect on our style and voice.

Scrutinize the work of your favorite author and see if you discover their style, or voice. Ask yourself, do my words mimic another writer's voice? And if so, does it mean you're guilty of copying their work intentionally or subliminally? The answer is *NO.* What are the chances of your words perfectly matching another writer's that you've read? We are individual in our thinking and individual in our writing—not plagiarists.

McKEE'S TEN COMMANDMENTS

1. Thou shalt not take the crisis/climax out of the protagonist's hands. The antideus ex machina commandment.

2. Thou shalt not make life easy for the protagonist. Nothing progresses in a story, except through conflict.

3. Thou shalt not give exposition for strictly exposition's sake. Dramatize it. Convert exposition to ammunition. Use it to turn the ending of a scene, to further the conflict.

4. Thou shalt not use false mystery or cheap surprise. Don't conceal anything important that the protagonist *KNOWS*. Keep us in step with the hero. We know what he/she knows. (Can know more, but not less.)

5. Thou shalt respect your audience. The anti-hack commandment.

6. Thou shalt know your world as God knows this one. The pro-research commandment.

7. Thou shalt not complicate when complexity is better. Don't multiply the complications on one level. Use all three: Intra-personal, Inter-personal, Extra-personal. (Conflict within, conflict between two people, conflict with/in society.)

8. Thou shalt seek the end of the line, the negation of the negation, taking characters to the farthest reaches and depth of conflict imaginable within the story's own realm of probability.

9. Thou shalt not write on the nose. Put a subtext under every text. (Depth, not simplified.)

10. Thou shalt rewrite.

TWO:
Things You Need To Know About Plot

The Story Setup

Decide What to Reveal

Keep to the point. Wandering narrative is less popular in today's fiction. The degree of narrative you include can be seen by the genre, and period of your setting. For example; a techno thriller will rely on action and a fast pace, while a historical nautical work of fiction will reveal events at a slower rate.

Having said this, we know that any given set of events will have more action and scene than can be told, or written. Describing every insignificant facet will result in a meandering, unwieldy and boring story, regardless of genre.

Yes, a glimpse into the scene is important, but avoid cluttering your reader's view with overstuffed furniture, voluminous velvet drapes, an alley filled with discarded empty beer cans, cigarette butts, an abandoned Jeep, a gang of stalking feral cats, and a Coors delivery truck.

Your audience must rely on your perspective and balance. Compare these examples:

FILM	PREMISE	WHAT ISN'T SAID
GONE WITH THE WIND	Life of plantation families in the American South.	The entire scope of the Civil War.
THE FIGHTER	A fighter from a hard-luck New England town rises to World Champion.	The details of the life of his major opponents.
SCHINDLER'S LIST	A group of Jews survive due to the efforts of an ambiguously heroic man.	The actual fighting of the war or the details about the allies.

Choose which aspects of your story add to the richness and texture, and which ones are mere diversions. Ask yourself: *"Is this detail important to the story?"*

What you include will send a message to your reader that it is a crucial piece of information. To quote Dr. Thomas M. Grundner, author, and founder of Fireship Press, *"In other words, don't let your words get in the way of the story."*

The Dumpster

Mark Twain once said, *"Sometimes you must kill your darlings."* And yes, this is as difficult as it sounds!

Say you describe what Johnny did at the playground in great depth, but it has nothing to do with the little girl who's been kidnapped. Your descriptions may be powerful; you share the color of daffodils and your reader can savor the pungent scent of springtime in the park through your evocations, but if little Johnny's play time isn't important to the story line, you must send it to the dumpster.

Make a file and name it *Notes*, or *Dumpster*, if you wish, and hide your orphaned darlings there to use at another time.

Choose What Not to Reveal

The art of withholding information is a powerful tool. An omniscient narrator won't have to worry about this. He knows everything, thus knows what not to tell.

But the first person, or limited narrator, must learn what information to hold back from his audience and when to divulge it later. For example:

FILM	PREMISE	WHAT ISN'T TOLD
STAR WARS	Luke must defeat Darth Vader.	Darth Vader is Luke's biological father.

Think about any novels, movies, or plays that have led you to perceive a situation to be a certain way, until the proper moment arrived when the writer unleashed the truth for maximum dramatic effect. It's potent stuff!

Author intrusion

This is another must-not-do. Don't bring your personal issues to the table of your reader. Say that you drift into your protagonist's head and find that he has the same opinion on gun control as you. Suddenly he agrees with you on every issue, and you are amazed and impressed by your character's keen insight. However, unless your readers share these same attitudes, you will lose them—and a reader is a terrible thing to waste.

Of course you will take appropriate issues to your character's platform, but do it wisely, and covertly.

Organizing Your Plot

Story Line

Your story must have structure. If not, you'll have a group of characters running amuck across the pages of your book, never in the right place at the right time, and you'll be painting yourself into every corner in sight. But how do you get your scenes and plot to be manageable?

There are as many methods as there are authors, but seldom do they rely on their own memory. Here are a few possibilities to help you keep track of the action.

Index Card Method: These are popular because of their mobility. Each time you create a character, list their vital statistics (*name, features, likes, dislikes*) on a card. As scenes begin to unfold, additional information can be placed on these cards. Ultimately, they can come together in an index file, or stacked on your desk, or spread out on the floor.

One advantage of this method is the sheer simplicity of cards. You can stick them in your pocket wherever you go and jot down ideas while away from your laptop or notebook.

Gathering unique names, such as from the name tag of a store clerk, describing the interior of a restaurant, or stealing from an overheard conversation, can be done with the least amount of notice. Color-coded cards work well for ease of identifying scenes or characters.

Plot Chart Method: You can design a "plot chart" for yourself or find examples on the Internet. A plot chart will divide scene development into sections containing a brief description, the characters involved, the time-frame, and anything else that helps you to carry the story forward in a structured, cohesive manner. In a sense, the sections of your chart can be seen as a series of mini-plots. They begin with a premise, contain plot development, set up a hook, sometimes meet with a resolution, and serve to propel the story forward.

Notebook Method: (The paper kind) Use a lined notebook with three holed pages that can transfer to a more organized binder. As with cards, your current project notebook goes everywhere with you.

1st line has the chapter number, day and/or time of the scene, and the location.

2nd line lists the main characters. You may want to color code these with highlighters to easily spot where they appeared last in the scheme of things.

3rd line contains main elements of the scene/plot along with anything else of importance, such as the first time a character appears.

> *Quick Tip*—When you go to the internet to do research, cut and paste entire articles that you might want to use all or part of later and store them in your '*Notes*' folder.

Computer Method: (No big surprise here) For the first draft keep each chapter in a separate file. Further down the road you can easily add, change, move or delete the files.

Once confident with your project, you will sense that your story line is well-developed, and you won't anticipate any major revisions.

Now combine these files into one document. This will enable you to see your word count, justify the alignment and insert page breaks and numbers.

> 'There are three rules for writing a novel. Unfortunately no-one knows what they are.'
>
> *Somerset Maugham*

Laws of Plotting

There are several elements that are necessary to the development of any work of fiction, whether it's a novella, fiction series, short story, or anecdote.

Some of these laws can be perceived as cyclical in nature; they are repeated from chapter-to-chapter, or scene-to-scene.

The Through-Line – *(aka Story Line, One-liner, Elevator pitch, What you say when someone asks about your book)*

Your manuscript must be drilled down to one or two dramatic sentences that contains a central conflict around which everything revolves, or evolves. Often this will pose a question such as:

When the girl encounters the serial killer, *will* she learn his evil plan in time to escape?

Here is one example of a through line from *The Midshipman Prince* by Tom Grundner:

> *How do you keep a prince alive when the combined forces of three nations (and a smattering of privateers) want him dead? Worse, how do you do it when his life is in the hands of a 17 year old lieutenant, an alcoholic college professor, and a woman who has fired more naval guns than either of them?*

As soon as possible, as you build your story idea, write a through-line and tack it somewhere in clear sight. It can be subject to change if your plot takes a new direction, (*check with your muse on this*), but keep it always before you.

Take a few minutes and give this a try. Aim for one to three sentences, and you may want to use a pencil with a good eraser, or plan on wearing out your Delete key.

Done? Congratulations! You have just mastered the art of reducing a 300 page, 100,000 word manuscript into a single sentence.

Good job, Houdini!

The First One Hundred Words

"Mama, are you a virgin?"

These words open the novel, *Coffee Will Make You Black,* by April Sinclair, and they represent the quintessential first words of a novel. What do these five words convey to us, the reader?

The speaker is young and less educated and likely a female who is bold and inquisitive.

The opening scene continues...

> *I was practicing the question in my head as I set the plates with the faded roosters down on the shiny yellow table. When Mama came back into the kitchen to stir the rice or turn the fish sticks or check on the greens, I would ask her.*
>
> *This afternoon at school a boy named Michael had passed me a note with "Stevie" written on it; inside it had asked if I was a virgin.*

This is how to get your readers attention. We've been let in on the narrator's name; Stevie, a look into her kitchen, and a bit of information about her mother. And we know why she is asking this question.

By following a dynamic set of key elements at the outset of your novel, you will entice a reader/shopper to reach for their credit card and buy your book.

How many times have you opened a book and perused just the first few paragraphs? Maybe on Amazon.com, or another online bookstore you have clicked on "Look Inside" to view these pages before you purchased? Maybe you're seeking a book with sixteenth century London as a setting, or New York City during the sixties.

Give your potential reader the information they want, and be specific.

> *Dana Coulter left the imposing building of the 9th precinct police complex in downtown Philadelphia.*
>
> *Her anger heightened at the sight of snarled rush hour traffic inching along Cedar. She brushed her auburn hair out of her eyes and fumbled with her umbrella, ready to face the freezing November rain.*
>
> *A voice from behind startled her—she knew who it was and anticipated the large filthy gloved hand even before it wrapped across her cheek and lips. With an insane rush of adrenaline, and without an ounce of remorse, she spun around and drove the four-inch tip of the umbrella into the groin of Hardy Bono.*
>
> *Then she hailed a taxi.*

With these first 112 words, I convey to the reader:

The scene begins outside of a police precinct in Philadelphia.

The protagonist's name, sex and hair color.

The time of day, month and the weather conditions.

Her mood.

Her immediate response to the attack.

The name of the antagonist.

The story is sure to be fast-paced.

The first 100 words of your work must catch your reader's attention and make them salivate for more.

Here is a charming opening paragraph from J. R. R. Tolkien's The Hobbit:

In a hole in the ground there lived a hobbit. Not a nasty, dirty, wet hole, filled with the ends of worms and an oozy smell, nor yet a dry, bare, sandy hole with nothing in it to sit down on or to eat: it was a hobbit-hole, and that means comfort.

Thus we know:

Who the story is about.

The setting is a hole in the ground.

You get a sense of smell and the setting.

In only 53 words the hook is set.

Define Your Genre

Choose a genre that fits your subject or concept.

Ask yourself how this genre meets your criteria.

Propose your subject audience, and target your word count.

A list of Fiction Genres

Your genre may change later, if that's okay with your muse, but do have some category in mind when you start. Next peruse a list of common genres, what they embody, and a suggested word count.

Finding a niche among these is daunting and you will find more lists on the Internet or in publications on writing fiction than you want to know about. Choose one that has credibility and you will learn there are few, if any, hard and fast rules.

The first thing you need to know is the difference between Literary and Mainstream titles. These are categories, not genres. In other words, you could write a literary children's classic, a mainstream political thriller, a literary high-fantasy, a mainstream cozy, or amateur sleuth.

LITERARY: Written with a philosophical view and cultured expression. Tends to be about human shortcomings. Not necessarily plot driven, but focused more on character traits and period.

Examples: John Updike, Sue Monk Kidd

Typical Length: 95,000—220,000 Words

MAINSTREAM: Novels written in everyday, less scholarly, language. Writing aimed at the widest audience and highest popularity.

Examples: James Patterson, Nicholas Sparks

Typical Length: 80,000 – 220,000 Words

Some will argue the following list of genres made popular by today's fiction market. To further convolute the issue, genres can be broken down into sub-genres, and sub-sub-genres.

CHILDREN'S:

Inspirational, Coming of age, Detective, Fantasy, Educational.

Examples: J.K. Rowling

Typical Length: 2,000 – 145,000 Words

MYSTERY

Who-dun-it. Crime, murder. It involves a puzzle that is solved by the protagonist thwarting the antagonist. This genre often includes a red-herring (*someone who leads suspicion away from the true criminal*).

Examples: Sue Grafton, James Patterson

Typical Length: 50,000 – 95,000 Words

Mystery Sub-genres:

Cozy or Amateur Sleuth: A traditional mystery with less violence. The puzzle is solved by a non-professional, i.e. an everyday person. Can include Chick/Hen Lit

Examples: Agatha Christie, Janet Evanovich

Typical Length: 60,000 – 95,000 Words

Hard-Boiled (noir): A private detective solves the crime through action and deduction.

Examples: Robert Crais, Stuart Woods

Typical Length: 80,000 – 100,000 Words

Police Procedural: Solved though law-enforcement officials, involving technical and investigative specialties and forensics. Has lots of action, blood and violence, and you can toss in a serial killer or stalker.

Examples: Ed McBain, Patricia Cornwell

Typical Length: 60,000 – 95,000 Words

(*Also can include: Caper, Historical, Legal, Series*)

ROMANCE

Conflict and resolution between a couple, often has a happy ending.

Romance Sub-Genres:

Romantic Suspense:	40,000 – 120,000
Historical:	40,000 – 95,000

Contemporary:	70,000 – 140,000
Series Romance:	80,000 – 140,000
Futuristic/Paranormal:	80,000 – 100,000
Inspirational/Christian:	80,000 – 120,000
Romantic Comedy:	40,000 – 70,000

(*Also may include: Chick/Hen Lit, Action/Adventure, Americana, American West, Erotica, Gothic*)

THRILLER

Conflict between a villain and the protagonist, against all odds, break-neck pace, extreme action. Often the reader knows who did it.

Examples: Richard A. Clarke, Dean Koontz

Typical Length: 65,000 – 75,000 Words

Thriller sub-genres include:

Conspiracy/Espionage: Situations arising from government secrecy and security, and the corrupting influence of power.

Examples: Robert Ludlum, Vince Flynn

Typical Length: 90,000 – 120,000 Words

Medical Thriller: Dean Koontz	80,000 – 120,000
Legal Thriller: John Grisham	80,000 – 120,000
Techno Thriller: Tom Clancy	90,000 – 120,000

(*Can include: Disaster, Eco-thriller, Treasure seeking, Adventure.*)

SPECULATIVE FICTION

Unrealistic in nature, from the imagination, utopian, alternate history, apocalyptic.

Examples: Ayn Rand, Orson Scott Card

Typical Length: 70,000– 120,000 Words

Science Fiction: Robert Sawyer	70,000– 120,000
Fantasy: Dennis McKiernan or Mercedes Lackey	60,000 – 200,000
Horror: Stephen King	90,000 – 120,000
Urban Fantasy Stephenie Meyer or Carrie Vaughn	80,000 – 120,000

WESTERN

Set in the American West, usually in the past, but current issues are also popular. They may include elements of the above genres.

Examples: Cormac McCarthy, Tony Hillerman, Sandi Ault, Michael Blake

Typical Length: 65,000 – 90,000 Words

YA – YOUNG ADULT

Includes many of the above themes set among teens.

Examples: Holly Black, Stephenie Meyer (*Twilight* Series), James Pattersen (*Maximum Ride* Series)

Typical Length: Word Count Varies

> *"...writing a novel is like driving a car at night. You can see only as far as your headlights, but you can make the whole trip that way."*
>
> E. L. Doctorow

Your Fiction Blueprint

ID the following each time you begin a new fiction project:

1. Write your premise.
2. Identify your protagonist. *(Have a chat with your protagonist and ask him/her questions. Have them write a letter to you. They'll reveal more information than you'll ever need or want to know, about who they are.)*
3. What are your protagonist's goals and needs?
4. Identify the inciting incident and obstacles.
5. Identify the antagonist.
6. What is the internal conflict with your antagonist and protagonist?
7. Identify the Major Characters.
8. Name some complications faced by all.
9. What is the time span of the story? The year, month and when will it end?
10. Where is your setting?
11. Outline your culmination, resolution and conclusion if possible.

THREE: Things You Need To Know About Setting, Place and Time

Creating a Vibrant Sense of Place and Time

The cast and characters of your story wait in the wings of the theater while you prepare a stage for them. You are the set director and it is *crucial* that you provide your audience with a *cinematic* sense of place and time.

What do you visualize in your mind's eye? If this isn't clear to you, I recommend that you consult with one of your characters. I took an interesting journey into this subject during the writing of *Listening to the Corn Grow*. The antagonist, Biggin Ray Bob Grady, took me by the hand and led me into Jubal's, the local watering hole where he spends too much of his time. He sat me down on an imaginary bar stool and went to join his buddies.

Leaning on the bar I observed the people, the surroundings and the action. I eavesdropped on muted or raucous conversations, listened to the clink of glasses and Patsy Cline's songs from an old jukebox. I inhaled cigarette smoke flavored by the scent of booze and testosterone cologne. My shoes got stuck on the floor from spilled whiskey and puke, and I downed a cold one.

Later in the story Ray Bob invited me to share his cell with him in the Nebraska State Penitentiary... and I did.

A classic example of a sense of place and time comes from writers like James Michener. His writing can be likened to the formation of a glacier. The plot often doesn't start until somewhere near the center of the book.

Tom Clancy is another author who shows us exactly where we are, but do we really need to know the number of bolts holding together a number ten hull panel of the USS *Theodore Roosevelt* nuclear-aircraft carrier? Nuts and bolts aside, Clancy is a great inspiration. During an interview with Writer's Digest Magazine, *January 2001,* he advised aspiring writers to *"...just tell the damned story"* whenever you are bogged down by over-thinking or during the editing process.

Today's readers value the opportunity to gain knowledge, and they invite limited amounts of info dumping. Let them in on descriptions that are new to them such as horse racing, fly fishing, or shopping at Rodeo Drive in Beverly Hills. It's up to you to know what provides a vivid sense of place and time, or what threatens to collapse a scene on the spot. But don't trick your reader. Write true. You may be read by a fly fisherman.

Your Place or Mine?

When selecting a novel to read, I check the first few pages to see where and when it takes place, how well done is the setting and do I feel lured into the scene.

Take again our opening 100 words with Dana Coulter in Philadelphia and the freezing rain, including the umbrella. We get the feeling we are standing next to her, or in her shoes.

If your setting exists in the real world, take care with identifying information. The locals will call you out if you get it wrong. A basic description will suffice, and then change up the names. Stores come and go, as do minor details, so create your own clever or whimsical names for streets and businesses. Add a cozy café, a street sign, a tree with a dog peeing on it, the deafening beat of the bass booming from a passing car. It's your imagination, driven by your muse.

People are shaped by their environment. Let the reader know where your characters live, work, and play, down to the private places in their life, such as the view from the porcelain throne.

Setting is Pivotal in Fiction

Setting to Character to Plot - one leads to the other in the natural flow of the story.

In his novel *Wicked,* Gregory Maguire writes an amazing opening prologue:

> *A mile above Oz, the Witch balanced on the wind's forward edge, as if she were a green fleck of the land itself, flung up and sent wheeling away by the turbulent air. White and purple summer thunderheads mounded around her. Below, the Yellow Brick Road looped back on itself, like a relaxed noose. Though winter storms and the crowbars of agitators had torn up the road, still it led, relentlessly, to the Emerald City. The Witch could see the companions trudging along, maneuvering around the buckled sections, skirting trenches, skipping when the way was clear. They seemed oblivious of their fate. But it was not up to the Witch to enlighten them.*

We find in these first 113 words the elements conducive to welcoming the reader into the scene. Whenever you feel at a loss for creating descriptive prose, read your favorite opening, or any other paragraph, for inspiration. He has set the scene and launched the story.

Here is another great example from the opening words of *Out of Africa*, by Isak Dinesen:

> *I had a farm in Africa, at the foot of the Ngong Hills. The Equator runs across these highlands, a hundred miles to the North, and the farm lay at the altitude of over six thousand feet. In the day-time you felt that you had got high up, near to the sun, but the early mornings and evenings were limpid and restful, and the nights were cold.*
>
> *...it was Africa distilled up through six thousand feet, like the strong and refined essence of the continent. The colours were dry and burnt, like the colours in pottery.*
>
> *...Nairobi was a motley place, with some fine new stone buildings, and whole quarters of old corrugated iron shops, offices and bungalows, laid out with long rows of Eucalyptus trees along the bare dusty streets.*

Ms. Dinesen gives us a vivid sense of place that leads to character and plot (action). Be bold, and willing to dig into insignificant bits, like a macro image, zoom in and see.

Pace

Stories differ in pace. A historical novel will tend to move at a slower meter. Action thrillers go non-stop. Whatever genre you select, the pace needs to be balanced. Many action plots take time out to breathe during a quiet night of romance, a funeral, or sleep. I call it taking time to smell the roses. Find the rhythm and the beat of your story and keep the pace in check.

Have you left the reader hanging from a cliff by his pinky finger? The essence of pace is to escalate or lower the speed, then hang them by their fingernails... then STOP. This automatically catapults the story forward. Every scene builds towards the final scene at the conclusion of the story. Your pace *must* move the action and the reader forward and culminate just in time. Know when to say *The End.*

Laws of Scene and Structure

Scene - Nonstop Action Set in one Place.

Before there can be dialogue and interaction between your characters, you must set up, or at least be aware of, the scene and structure where the action takes place. Your reader gets settled in and becomes a spectator in your theater. This is not all that different from your plot chart, but is more focused on the *where* than the *how*.

Place - A room, office, hospital, police station... briefly identifies the opening words of your scene, by either narrative or through the eyes and dialogue of your character. As the story continues, you add more depth and texture to the place.

Time - Season, month, day, hour, holiday... are immediately shown in the opening.

Why - The event...what brought these people or this person to the scene.

Action - Movement, dialogue, interaction...the scene being played out.

Crisis - Rather than the entire scope of your premise and inciting incident that the book is based on, this is specific to this single scene. It is a lessor incident.

Culmination - Each scene has a high point and this is the mini-hook that carries the reader to the next scene (or chapter).

Resolution - Also part of our cyclical analogy, and can be a partial resolution. A small problem gets solved, but another comes into play.

At the conclusion of a scene, we want the reader to think about what has transpired and look forward to what comes next.

Show Versus Tell

Is a picture worth a thousand words? Not in fiction!

Other than POV (Point of View), this is the thorniest lesson for new writers to grasp. Reword this statement and repeat it every time you write. *A word is worth a thousand pictures!*

Showing versus Telling

Consider the opening paragraphs of my short story "Miranda of Luckenbach". Instead of simply *telling* the reader the setting, the author provides an example of how we can *show* through narrative as well as dialogue.

This would be telling:

> *Luckenbach is in the southeastern county of Gillespie Texas, has a population of three, and a permanent ghost. A narrow dust-pocked road turns at a sharp angle where Miranda sits combing her hair. Many men were hung from the hanging tree at the entrance to town, but Miranda was purposely drowned.*

One night she tried to prevent a biker from being terrorized by a group of crusty ghosts who to this day haunt the old tree. Once she was in love with a boy named Byron... before she died... when they were in high-school.

This is Showing:

Luckenbach: population three living souls, an assortment of chickens, and one permanent ghost... me, lies hidden beneath a full moon just thirteen miles from Fredericksburg in southeastern Gillespie County, Texas. It sets between South Grape Creek and Snail Creek, off of U. S. Highway 290. That's where you come to Luckenbach Town Loop Road...

Late last Tuesday night a biker came sputtering down the road into town. There wasn't any moon and the town was blacker than the middle of a cat's eye. I'd bet he's looking for a place to bed down.

Up ahead of him homeless Harvey was hanging out at the tree, hoping to scare the crap out of someone.

Biker Dude was kinda cute, so I hopped on behind him and tried to steer him the other way. No luck.

That poor boy totally freaked out when he pulled to the side of the road about fifteen feet from the hanging tree, and old ugly Harvey swung down and wrapped his legs around biker boy's neck...

I have a little more class, as ghosts go. Whenever I walk the Loop Road of Luckenbach at night, I wear a fancy saloon dress and only target drunks...

Giving up on my hair, I scoot further out on the limb and dangle my feet in the creek. Byron loved my hair—among other things. One day we got naked and hid in a field of bluebonnets. We kissed and played. He picked a handful of wild flowers, showered them across my bare belly, sucked a dandelion from my navel and ate it. "You and me and dandelion wine..." he sang.

It's easy to see the texture, emotions and life that come from showing the story (even of a playful ghost).

Laws of Show and Tell

1. Telling is shallow and boring.
2. Showing takes the reader inside of the story, from one-dimensional to three-dimensional.
3. Showing reveals motives and intention.
4. Showing connects the reader through the senses.
5. Showing reveals the voice and dialogue of the characters.
6. Showing gives the reader a sense of time and place, especially if the story is set in an unfamiliar place or time.
7. Showing deepens the suspense.
8. Showing helps the reader to understand relationships.
9. Showing heightens expectations of what comes next.
10. Showing makes the story real for the reader.
11. Never use an adjective or adverb unless it is necessary. This will strengthen your sentences and allow you to show rather than tell.
12. Don't over-describe. Write clear, succinct sentences to create a clearer picture.
13. Don't over-dramatize a scene. It's one thing if your protagonist is a drama queen, and another to carry emotions to the point of melodrama.

Try this... Write a short scene following the laws of Show vs Tell. Put to work each of your senses and include them in the your characters life.

Now change this paragraph/scene, by removing any adverbs and adding stronger verbs. Then do the same to the following sentences:

She spoke rapidly.
He slowly walked through the park.
The steak was overly cooked.

Clip your Clichés

cli·che \klē-ˈshā, ˈklē-ˌ, kli-ˈ\ **cliché** *adjective*

1. a trite phrase or expression; also the idea expressed by it.
2. a hackneyed theme, characterization, or situation.
3. something (as a menu item) that has become overly familiar or commonplace.

Common place and overused slang, sayings, jargon, and talk are what clichés are made of. The conundrum arises from the way we talk today. Our sentences are chock full of these expressions, thought to be the latest style. But fads grow old real fast.

As a rule of thumb, we want to test everything we write to see if some of these culprits have snuck in without us knowing. The exception might come in dialogue. But don't overdue this. It gets jangling on the ears of the reader.

Buzz words that are popular are okay to use, sparingly. But really, be honest, there is the danger that this will date your story, unless that's what you're going for. Today's buzz words will be tomorrow's clichés.

Pop Quiz:

How many clichés are in the above three paragraph?

What are a few other irritating, time-worn, cliches you can name?

> *"The plot and characters dance a sinister tango, entangling and weaving themselves into a story. And then the details come raining down."*
>
> Jaqueline Girdner

FOUR:
Things You Need To Know About Characterization

Character Development

When developing a character, you need to get to know him/her before you introduce them to your reader. To start your plot chart you'll need to have a basic personality in mind. You may not know these people's names yet, but if you find out later that the name isn't a good fit, you can always change it.

Let's get the introductions over with and we'll flesh out your characters as we go:

PROTAGONIST – Main character. What if your story begins with two strong lead characters? In time one will rise above the other. Do you have an inanimate protagonist? In a child's story about a sail boat, the inanimate boat becomes the main character or protagonist.

ANTAGONIST – The bad guy. Or in your sail boat plot, a hurricane may be the antagonist.

MAJOR CHARACTERS – These remain throughout the plot of the story and are integral to the role of your protagonist and antagonist.

MINOR CHARACTERS – These people (or animals, or things) come and go, and may or may not have names or detailed descriptions. They are given a short but important role.

WALK-ONS – These are background characters, or extras in the movie world. They hang around in the wings and get paid very little, if anything, other than a free meal from the concessionaire.

When developing your plot chart, try to identify the top three above. Like we said, you can change them later, add more, or kill your darlings. Once you've passed the introduction of you character, try holding a conversation with them.

> *"Every human being has hundreds of separate people living under his skin. The talent of the writer is his ability to give them their separate names, identities, personalities, and have them relate to other characters living with him."*
>
> Mel Brooks

How Writers Get to Know Their People

Have your character write a letter to you in which they share specifics about their life.

Here is a list of possibilities, but you'll want to modify it to fit your story's needs. Getting to know your characters is a lot like dating. On the first date you keep it simple and focus on physical attributes and making a good impression. As time goes along you'll learn the following:

Date and place of birth
Childhood history
Schools, degrees, skills
Intelligence
Work history
Parents and siblings
Mate and children
Present location
Present occupation
Political affiliations
Major accomplishments
Talent, humor
Difficult issues during life (divorce, surgery, etc.)
Any infirmities and disabilities, general health
Flaws, habits and anything unique
Favorite: Color
  Actors
  Movies
  Plays
  Music
  TV Shows
  Sports
  Public figures
  Styles
Favorite historical figures
Mannerisms, body type, body language
Friends, peers
Moral and ethical values
Preferences
Goals, motivations, dreams

Now it's your turn to ask them questions and write down their answers for future reference, such as what cologne or perfume do they prefer, or what foods do they hate, and what allergies do they have? You get the idea.

Observe or talk with your own friends or acquaintances who have similar traits and lifestyles as your character. This is especially helpful in learning about a person's occupation, style of dress and the jargon they use at their industry specific job.

It's your job to know your lead characters inside and out: Their flaws, their secret thoughts, what's inside of their refrigerators, or the brand and style of their underwear. Do they have nervous mannerisms? Weird habits? Who is the most important person in their life?

Where else can we find these *Real* folks to portray in our characters? People-watch wherever you go: at work, school, the park, spa, on a train, in an airport. Then visit their hangouts: a basketball court, exercise club, bookstore, or art gallery. Pick someone there to be your pseudo-character. We can project ourselves into their situation and ask: How would I feel? What would I say? Then instill your character's passions, thrills or fears into your reader's life.

It's possible you may want to set up an interview or an appointment with someone in the same field or industry as your character. Ask for a few minutes of their time, and if they would allow you to follow them as they go through their business day or perform their working skills. Take notes, photos and recordings (if they allow).

Note to Self...

Have my protagonist and one or two of my major characters write a letter to me, using the lessons of characterization.

Is your character round and three-dimensional? They must be complex and possess conflicting traits. It's possible for a person to be:

Frivolous but responsible.

Slovenly yet dependable.

Conservative yet daring.

A flat character is shallow and always predictable. They are stereotypes, like the shifty-eyed thief and the anorexic model.

> "I have no influence over them *(the characters).* I'm only an observer, recording. The story is always being told by the characters themselves."
>
> Erskine Caldwell

A Name Paints a Thousand More Pictures

Look at names in a telephone book or online for lists of names: male, female, last names, by country of origin, and more. Choose a tough name for a street fighter, a classy name for a female reporter, a weak name for a coward or a scandalous name for a scoundrel. My antagonist, Biggin Ray Bob Grady in *Listening to the Corn Grow,* is identified and defined by how he dresses, his tastes in women, food, and of course by his name.

The name you select for your character must fit the role, and above all be memorable.

John, Joe, Sue, Ann are *NOT* memorable by name alone. That's not to say they can't be incredible in their roles, but it helps to label them well. Avoid names beginning with the same first letter. It can be frustrating to your reader if you pick names beginning with the same letter for say five sisters: Betty, Barbara, Bella, Beth or Brittany. These girls may be well-defined through their character development, but there will be confusion throughout the story because of these similar names, no matter what.

Start a list. It's easy to find unique monikers wherever we go. What first comes to mind when you hear these names?

Ted Dishman	Zoey Osmond
Martin Notorangeli	Alexander Richardson
Claudia Felici Regis	Dorrington Mud
Manny Tosca	Drexel Rose

What is your first thought when you hear these well-known names?

Scarlett and Rhett	Zorro
James Bond	Tom Brady
Simon Cowell	Shrek
Winston Churchill	Madonna

Ask your characters:

What do they most fear?

What is their motivation in overcoming obstacles?

What do they stand to lose?

Where will they turn for advice, knowledge or skill and how can they equip themselves?

How much are they invested?

Have them finish this sentence—*If I could...*

Laws of building Solid Characters

The five senses: Let your reader be a part of your characters five senses. How does an infant son feel to its mother...his scent, sound and taste? From *Listening to the Corn Grow:*

"Lil takes Mattie's hand between her lips and runs her tongue over his fingertips tasting remnants of banana pudding, and watches him as he giggles with delight."

Sensory Experiences: You get to be responsible for conveying these sensory experiences to your reader. You want them to taste the pudding, feel the pain, hear the wind.

Indelible identity: Choose a name that fits your character's personality.

Be Unique! This is again, a VITAL law. As in scene and description, it's your job to think up new ways to say old things about people. Fads will date your story and your characters. Sky blue eyes is cliché'd, eyes the shade of thunder clouds is unique, but a bit corny. Try... his eyes spoke of indigo nights. You get the idea.

Listen to your Characters: They will whisper secrets in your ear and flaunt who they are.

Use a Thesaurus: This will transform your:

NORMAL: ordinary, commonplace, usual, regular, everyday, run of the mill, average mundane... words into:

EXTRAORDINARY: astonishing, peculiar, exceptional, amazing, unexpected... prose.

Flesh Out Your Characters

FLESH OUT: to put flesh on the bones of. Give substance to, provide with details, amplify.

You need to put flesh on the bones of your characters. It's an expression you will hear often in the writing world. It reiterates the idea that we give our reader the whole character, from emotional, to intellectual to physical. They must be three-dimensional, multi-faceted, have layers that run deep, have clear identities, be unique, and believable, and above all...

The reader must care what happens to them!

> **Note to self...**
>
> *I must continue to throw obstacles at, and generally plague my protagonist with overlapping hurdles...more is better. He/she and some of the major characters, must work at getting through this adventure alive, and maybe save the world as well.*

FIVE:
Things You Need To Know About Dialogue, Voice and Point of View

What is Voice?

How do we define the mystery of voice in fiction?

Voice is a puzzling term to new writers. Simply said, voice comes from inside your head and onto the pages you write.

In fiction you'll have the voice of the narrator and the voices of your characters. The more you know your character, the better you'll hear their voice.

> *"Each piece of dialogue must be "something happening... The "amusing" for its own sake should, above all, be censored... The functional use of dialogue for the plot must be the first thing in the writer's mind. Where functional usefulness cannot be established, dialogue must be left out."*
>
> Elizabeth Bowen

Some Does and Don'ts:

DO use active rather than passive verbs *(was making him sick, felt disturbing to me. "Emmy dropped the glass"* is active; *"the glass was dropped"* is passive*)*

DON'T use awkward verbs *(have, appeared, exist)*

AVOID weak, inert verbs (The scent of rotten fish *was making him sick*..The scent of rotting fish *made me feel completely sick.)*

DO use potent, present, active verbs. *(run/chase, hit/strike, complain/bitch)*

DO use slang, local dialect or accents discreetly. If your character is from Louisiana—or any locale that has a distinct sound—it's okay to include this in early conversation, but play it down as you progress. Jargon and dialect will keep the character unique, but can detract from the potency of the dialogue or narrative.

How do you know if you're writing in a skillful voice? Try reading your work out loud. Awkward and stilted words will beg to be rewritten.

Ya'll and *reckon* does not a Southerner make. You need to search the elements of the dialect, grammar, syntax and word choice to make it authentic. Break the mold. It's okay to use misspelled words. Here is an example from Norman Mailer's *The Naked and the Dead:*

> *Ridges laid down his shovel and looked at him. His face was patient but there was some concern in it. "What you trying to do, Stanley?" he asked.*
>
> *"You don't like it?" Stanley sneered.*
>
> *"No, sir, Ah don't."*
>
> *"Aah, fug it," he said, turning away.*

Mailer said that the use of obscenities was unfashionable during that period, therefore, changing the spelling helped. Again, it's not necessary to make every sentence sound local, but you can toss in a word or two occasionally to keep the person in character.

Body language is another aspect of *Voice*. Expressions like; *lowered his eyes, cocked her head to one side, licked her lips, bounded along,* can flesh out the character's personality, their conversation, and add visual depth.

Seamless Dialogue Moves Your Story Forward

Dialogue as a Vehicle

Dialogue is more than the words publishers enclose in quotation marks, and follow up with *he said, she said.* It's the bond that pulls together information. Dialogue is one of the tools we use to show rather than tell.

Here is another example.

Without dialogue, the following is flat, and results in telling rather than showing. From my novel *The Spaghetti Wars*, we read:

> *By nine-thirty Zoey and I had had enough shopping-bag-therapy to last until next Black Friday and we had the packages to prove it. We hailed a taxi and returned to the restaurant. Rospo's was already closed for the night, but a few regulars still nursed their booze of choice and gazed at ESPN.*
>
> *Vincenzio, the head waiter, offered to take our bags. We stomped the snow from our boots and hung our jackets in the coat room. It was clear that the storm would prevent both Zoey and me from driving to our respective homes. Vincenzio asked us if we needed a room, but I had a better idea. We'd visit Mama Rosa.*

Use of dialogue:

"I'm exhausted. I've had enough shopping-bag-therapy to last until next Black Friday," I said, struggling against the snow and wind.

"And we've got the packages to prove it," Zoey responded. It was ten at night and the stores in downtown Boston were closing.

We had walked to town from the restaurant, before the storm hit. With my head lowered against the onslaught, I began waving my hand in the air. "There has to be an empty taxi out here somewhere," I yelled.

A Boston Checkered Cab pulled to the curb and the driver loaded our bags. "Where to, ladies?"

"Il Rospo Siciliano Restaurant, over on Hanover."

"Good evening Gray, Zoey, I see you women outdid yourselves. Let me give you a hand," Vincenzio, our head waiter offered, as we set our burgeoning shopping bags in a booth. Although Rospo's was closed for the night, a few of the regulars still nursed their booze of choice and watched ESPN. We stomped snow from our boots, and hung our jackets in the coat room.

"Now what?" Zoey asked. "I'm not sure either of us should be driving home tonight. The roads are miserable."

"You've got a point. My nerves won't take plowing my car through this storm for over an hour," I said.

We wandered into the dim light of the dining room now filled with ghosts of today's patrons, and I pulled aside one of the thick window drapes. Wind carried crystal particles in drifts across the empty street.

"I love the scent of garlic, marinara sauce and wine mixed with smoke from the fireplace," I said. My reverie was interrupted by Vincenzio.

"You ladies need a room?" he asked, pretending not to be eavesdropping.

"Um, no, I have a better idea." I grabbed Zoey's arm. "Let's go upstairs and see if Mama Rosa is still awake. She has a couple of sofas. We'll camp out with her tonight."

In this example we have two scenes, one in downtown Boston, the second at Rospo's Italian restaurant. But rather than telling about these places or the dilemma that Gray and Zoey face as in the first selection, the details are divulged through their dialogue.

How difficult is it to pen proper dialogue? Some will assert that it's the trickiest part of writing. But think about it, we engage in conversation daily, and we have internal speech (our voice). Why not write the same way? Like Vincenzio, we need to eavesdrop on our characters conversations.

Compare this to public speaking. Envision your readers to be a small group you are standing before, ready to address. Have you prepared? Do you know your subject inside and out? If so, you'll feel confident and your speech will come across natural, genuine and sincere. It will be real. But if you haven't prepared, your audience is going to feel uncomfortable, be put off, and walk out.

Dialogue Structure

With dialogue comes the necessity of quotes, commas, who said what to whom, and where? The moment a character opens their mouth to speak, or allows us into their brain to share thoughts, we need to know exactly who they are. A change in speaker is usually indicated by a new paragraph.

Ellipsis points may be used if there is a halting in the speech, such as: *"No... no... Oh my God, it can't be true."* It's acceptable to use quotations in internal dialogue, but the norm is to write this in italics. There is nothing objectionable about *he said, she said.* In fact, as we read, we seldom notice these words. Try it. Your eyes will skim over them, moving on to the heart of the conversation.

Be careful HOW they say it:

"Darling, those shoes are stunning," she gushed.

"What the hell is that?" he exploded.

If your sentence speaks to the reader with enough emotion or strength, you can skip the gushing and exploding. *Stunning and hell* are sufficient to make the point.

Some authors today have decided that the word '*said*' is boring. To prove how clever *(and amateurish)* they are, they invent what editors and critics often refer to as melodramatic dialogue or *bookisms.* Here is my example:

> *"Danny, hurry the hell up, the cops will be here before we can disappear the body," Annie* ***growled*** *in a hushed voice.*
>
> *"Don't go weirding out on me, Ann, I need you to get the lid off the damned box, and do it fast. I can't stand here all night holding up this dick-head. Once we get him sealed in the crate, he'll be flying off on the next cargo plane," Danny* ***snapped****, glancing around the darkened warehouse, wishing Annie would pay attention to prying loose the stubborn lid.*
>
> *"Look, who's the real dick-head in this room, the living or the dead?" Annie* ***blurted****, "I mean it, you've been acting like this is all my fault. It wasn't me that stuck this guy in the freezer," she* ***mumbled,*** *grunting from the effort of prying at the box.*
>
> *"No, but it is your fault that he showed up here in the first place. Shit, Annie, we gotta get out of here or we'll end up as cold and stiff as he is." Danny* ***spat*** *the words at her, like she was an idiot.*
>
> *"This lid won't budge," she* ***whined****. Holding the crowbar in the air, she swung it in circles until she finally shot back at Danny her true feelings. Leaning*

forward, crowbar poised above his head, she articulated her next words with the venom of a snake, "Here, lay the body on the floor and take this," she ***hissed.***

He dropped the body, grabbed the raised crowbar from Annie with one hand and slapped her out of the way with the other. "Fine, Bitch," he **chuckled**. *He gave her a menacing look and* **snickered**, *"I'll get the box open, and then I'll deal with you."*

Now read this dialogue once again, changing the underlined words to *'said'*. You'll see how the spoken words and the actions stay strong without the *bookisms*.

Rather than embellish a conversation, these *bookisms* often draw the reader away from the action, or maybe the tension of the moment.

Whenever you are tempted to toss in a *bookism*, ask yourself what words you can use to strengthen the dialogue itself. This doesn't mean you should never use an expression, or dialogue tag. Treat them like special delicacies, to be indulged in on occasion.

Allow your character to *shout or whisper*, but would they really *thunder, splutter, snort, grunt, or ejaculate* their words? In certain situations they may *plead, or giggle,* especially when coupled with action. But, *ejaculate*? And this comes from an actual text, which I will not identify further.

As for punctuation, there's Cormack McCarthy, and then there's the rest of us. He uses few speech marks, apostrophes, colons, semi-colons and his sentences are clipped and sparse.

Take a look at his novel *The Road*. You'll find that his brilliance is found in verse that is crisp, fresh and precise. Try taking this style to an agent or publisher. It won't happen. We have to abide by the rules until the day comes that we are worthy of casting our own style onto pages and eBooks.

Every line of dialogue should do three things...move the story forward, disclose character, and sound realistic. Keep it succinct, and don't let your people make chit-chatter or deliver long speeches. And use proper punctuation.

Give it a try... Take a few minutes, invent a couple of characters, and have them start a conversation. Use proper punctuation, and follow the rules above.

To write dialogue is a powerful God-like phenomenon. You become the creator, molding your characters, and breathing life into them as they converse with one another.

Qualifier and Modifier

A qualifier is a word that affects the meaning of another, usually describing it or restricting its meaning. These are true adverb and adjectives, such as *red* in *"I love Cody's new red car."* Seldom are these a problem in dialogue.

On the other hand, a Modifier is a word or phrase that increases or decreases the quality signified by the word (adjective, adverb) it modifies.

A few of these modifiers are *very, all, somewhat, quite, rather, more, just, lot, still, a bit, a little, a great deal, sort of, pretty, almost, fairly.* (This is not a hard and fast rule, because at times these words have other important functions.)

Here is an example: *"The wind was very strong."* The word *very* does little to tell us how strong the wind is. If we want to heighten the drama, say: *"The wind raged at gale force."*

Useless modifiers are used to expand or limit a meaning. In reality, these can weaken the sentence. Your six characters are planning to travel together in a compact vehicle, and Carla realizes there won't be enough room:

*"We **all** crowded into the compact vehicle and that's when I realized there wasn't enough room for our luggage," Carla said...vs.*

"We crowded into the compact vehicle and that's when I realized there wasn't enough room for our luggage," Carla said.

In the second illustration, the reader doesn't question how many, or did they *all* crowd in; it is irrelevant. Well chosen nouns, verbs, adjectives and adverbs do a better job. They make our writing, and dialogue more precise, vital, crisp and unique. The better the adjective, and the well-placed adverb we choose, the less need we have for a modifier or a qualifier. It results in dialogue (and narrative) that is fluid and seamless.

Keeping in Character With Dialogue

This being said, if our character insists on throwing in:

"Alex almost always says to me that hardly ever do all of them do just a little bit of tidying up around the house, I pretty much can't openly accuse them of basically lying their asses off, and eventually even they simply will have to truly admit that they are all just slackers." (Okay, so this is overkill.)

But the point is illustrated by: "Alex says no one tidies up the house, and they need to admit they are slackers."

JUNK Words and TRASHY Habits

About	Almost	Already
Am	Appear	Approximately
Are	As	Basically
Been	Being	Close to
Even	Eventually	Exactly
Exist	Finally	Mostly
All	Has	Have
Here	Just	Just then
Kind of	LY words	Now
Practically	Really	Seems
Somehow	Somewhat	Sort of
That	Truly	Very
Was	Were	

AVOID - *ING*' words. They tend to make a sentence weak

CAUTION - Did you know *that that* word on *that* list could be replaced?

AVOID - the above *Junk Words* by strengthening your verbs and nouns.

EXCEPTIONS - to this can be found in dialogue.

AVOID - repeating words in close proximity. Use your thesaurus to replace words, rather than repeat them. The sound of repetition will stand out when you read out loud.

POV—Point of View

Another weighty task with writing fiction is to stay within the point of view of the character who owns a scene..Who is telling or experiencing the story? STAY in that Point of View throughout a scene.

First-person POV

This is the most natural POV, since in the real world we view life from an "I" perspective. We're aware of first-person when a character narrates the story with *I-me-my-mine* in his or her speech.

In this POV you get to hear the thoughts of the character and see the story through his/her eyes. The narrator is allowed to know things that the character does not. Take Scout, a young girl in Harper Lee's *To Kill a Mockingbird,* told in her POV. She doesn't grasp the complex racial and socioeconomic relations of her town—but the reader does, because Scout gives information that the reader can interpret.

The following sample is again taken from my *The Spaghetti War.* This is written from Ruby Jeans' POV. Although we switch to action involving her mother Hanna, who is further away from where Ruby stands, we don't convert to her mother's POV. It is Ruby who sees the action, and relates what her mother says.

> *Steam appeared from a sludgy grate in the cracked cement sidewalk and it felt warm on my frozen legs. I was waiting for my mother to emerge from a broken window in the basement of an old building. We had spent the last two hours keeping warm in the Boston Public Library. Now it was after nine, the library had closed its doors, and like other*

homeless, we needed to find a place to sleep. I squinted through the mist at the outline of our bright red SUV, one of the few remainders of our other life.

I remembered the afternoon last August when Dad and I went shopping for an SUV for Mom's birthday. I thought it was an odd gift. Mom always got us fun presents. But not Dad...he was practical.

"Ruby Jean, come on down here," my mother called from the dark alley.

"Mom, we can sleep in the car. I like it there." I peered around the corner and saw my mother's head sticking out from a basement window about five feet below the alleyway. She was wearing her Mary Poppins hat. I hated it.

She insisted, "No, not the van. I've found a good place down here in this basement, and we're supposed to get several inches of snow tonight. Help pull me out of here and we'll move our bedding inside."

"Fine," I muttered. I left the warmth of the grate, traced my way down the alley and leaned over an iron rail with my hand outstretched to my Mother, Hanna Argolin Richardson.

She wriggled through the window and together we grabbed blankets and pillows from the SUV and dumped them into the basement of what looked to be a large Italian restaurant. I could smell meatballs... my tummy growled.

Are you in a character's head, immersed in a scene? It is easy to slip from one POV to another without realizing it until you get the writing side of your brain to understand that this *is not allowed.* It is *mandatory* that you know who's POV you are in. It is incumbent on you to keep this focus.

Advantage of First-person POV

- It is subjective.
- The reader always knows who is seeing the action.
- You can choose a voice more freely.
- In first-person you may use slang, bad grammar, etc., while third-person restricts you to Standard English.
- First-person allows free access to what the person is thinking.

Disadvantages of First-person

- Dialogue is more difficult to incorporate.
- We can't see the person, because they can't see themselves. But they can be told how they look by another character, or glimpse themselves in a reflection.
- It's not as easy to stay in this POV for an entire story, although many writer's and best-sellers are successful at it.
- In first-person we must stay within this persons parameters. For example, your character has no knowledge of what is happening off scene, other than through telephone, television, internet, or someone telling them first hand.
- The other option is to switch POV in a new chapter or scene, but this can confuse your reader if not handled with discretion.
- When can we switch POV? At the completion of a scene, but it's best to let the reader know by adding a signal, such as 'rabbits', those little asterisks that separate sections.

***

And you may change POV at the completion of a chapter or section, such as Part 1.

Third-person POV

This is when we, the creator, write *"he"* *"she"* or *"they"*, rather than *"I"*. This POV requires further choices. You, the writer get to choose between:

Third-person Omniscient Where we know everything about every one of our characters, including the places and the events placed in our scenes. This is sometimes refered to as the *"God's-eye"* view. We can observe from many angles, similar to a camera.

Third-person Subjective POV resembles first-person, but done in Standard English in the voice of a narrator, rather than character voice. Example: *"As Carrie watched fitness infommercials on T.V., she thought about working out more often."* Here we see from her eyes AND we have access to her thoughts.

Third-person Objective where we can see what our character is doing without getting inside of her head and we don't see this situation from anyone else's POV. This is like what a camera sees, but you don't see the cameraman.

"As Carrie watched infommercials, she made a grocery list."

Third-person Limited Omniscient POV or Third-person Flexible POV here the objective and the subjective approaches are combined:

"As Carrie watched infommercials on TV, she made a grocery list and remembered that her mother wanted her to buy milk." We can see Carrie and read her thoughts.

Last comes Second-person POV

In Second-person POV, the author makes believe he is talking to someone, describing what the person addressed is doing.

This gets tricky because the "you" is not the reader. Example:

...your hands tremble as you knock on the door; you'd rather be safe and warm at home. Sleet melts from your eyebrows, but you are determined to confront Edward.

In second-person, the narrator directs the story to another character using *you*; the story is being told through the teller's point of view. Second person is the least commonly used POV in fiction.

> Coleridge was a drug addict. Poe was an alcoholic. Marlowe was stabbed by a man whom he was treacherously trying to stab. Pope took money to keep a woman's name out of a satire; then wrote a piece so that she could still be recognized anyhow. Chatterton killed himself. Byron was accused of incest.
>
> Do you still want to be a writer—and if so, why?
>
> Bennett Cerf
> Co-founder of Random House

Have Some Fun With POV

Create a scene in first person POV that features a grade school teacher and her student as your characters. They live in an economically poor back-woodsy area and speak with a heavy local accent. They are involved in an argument about why the student needs to be in class on time every day. Use the things we've studied about *Voice, Dialogue and POV.* Then compare your example with the following Laws of Voice, Dialogue and Point of View:

Laws of Voice, Dialogue & POV

Avoid weak verbs.

Use slang, dialect and accents discreetly.

Body language adds to voice.

Use dialogue to show rather than tell.

Do keep you dialogue in true conversation quality.

You must know your characters intimately to capture believable dialogue.

Whichever POV you choose for your fiction, you MUST stay true to it, as you do with tense.

Do use active verbs.

SIX:
Things You Need To Know About Resolution and Research

Denouement, Conclusion, Epilogue

The *Resolution* is where we get together with our characters and solve the problems that have carried us through the previously described action and crises. It's where the questions that are posed during the story are answered.

Will our heroine save the day? How? Who lives, and who dies? Who laughs, and who cries? The cyclical mini-resolutions that we've positioned at the end of scenes or chapters now come together in a culmination.

Liken this to a roller coaster ride:

We have the rising action (*the inciting incident*) as we climb higher and higher.

Down we go on an adventure that leads to more hills (*of conflict*) and dips (*lesser resolutions*),

Until we swing through another curve, mount one last obstacle (*the crises, culmination*), hang for a moment, poised and ready, then dip to a slow smooth stop (*the conclusion, final resolution*).

Until the end comes, you need to keep your readers on the edge. This won't work if you've given out too much prior information through action and character. Doing this will cause the resolution to appear redundant.

A realistic conclusion can be accomplished in several ways:

- Through the natural process of dialogue and action as our characters overcome the climactic obstacles they face. This could take several scenes or chapters.
- A mixture of narrative, dialogue and action can take your reader through the conflict and resolution.
- In a story written in first person, the speaker is the one who generally divulges the resolution as we follow their life.
- Omniscient narrative is appropriate in some instances—when everyone else in the scene is dead or gone.

> *'If you are going to make a book end badly, it must end badly from the beginning.'*
>
> Robert Louis Stevenson

The Wrap

This is a commonly known movie term that sheds information and perspective on what has taken place. This is what a denouement consists of, putting the pieces of your story together and coming to a smooth conclusion.

The Epilogue

A story may conclude with a harrowing rescue scene. We've learned who survived and who didn't make it, and we know how they were rescued.

The crises and conclusion are complete and the scene ends with your protagonist and characters standing dripping wet on a deserted beach.

Do you, the author, leave them shivering in the cold?

With the epilogue, you have the opportunity to tie up the loose ends, such as letting the reader know what happened when they returned home. How did the adventure affect their future?

It's common to make a short gap in time from when the action stopped to the epilogue. Call it a resolution, if you will, to the conclusion.

What do you want your readers to remember? How do they feel as they read the final sentence? Happy? Sad? Moved? Inspired?

The conclusion, or epilogue, gives you the opportunity to instill this in your readers.

As your reader closes the book, or powers off his e-reader, he will remember five things:

The hook
The vivid sense of place and time
The unique characters
The plot
And the conclusion.

But... will they?

The Circular Ending

Endings give an answer to the earliest questions posed, as far back as the initial hook. They tie together the questions and answers.

But a circular ending uses an early paragraph that is repeated at, or near, the end.

For example a story opens with the main character eating at a sleazy Los Angeles restaurant. He overhears the bartender say that nothing exciting ever happens in this place. Minutes later a shooting occurs and our character is drawn into a chain of uncanny, diabolical events. Two days later, he's back in the same booth having lunch again.

Matching v. Non-matching Ending

Similar to a circular ending, a matching ending answers the original premise. A non-matching ending involves a different set of characters and protagonist. The original people have been replaced, perhaps due to length of time, or death.

Surprise Ending

Then there's the O'Henry ending. For example, we might be duped by a red-herring—something or someone placed in the story to throw the reader off track, and only at the very end is the surprising truth revealed.

In Who-done-it mysteries, everything possible is done to mislead the reader. You may drop subtle hints, but never divulge enough information to allow them to solve the mystery until you choose the time.

Trick Ending

The resolution and final actions will lead the reader to believe the story is over. Bam! It turns out there's more to it than we realized.

Summary Ending

This is where you use narrative to *tell* your audience the ending. Tom Wolfe successfully uses a summary ending for *The Bonfire of the Vanities*. But wouldn't you rather *show* your readers the end through scene and dialogue?

Open Ending

Allows your readers to come to their own conclusion as to how things turned out for your protagonist and characters. Here is an example of an open ending:

A Gunfight is the title of a movie set in a Mexico border town where Johnny Cash and Kirk Douglas appear as retired gunfighters who are goaded by the townsfolk into a duel or final shoot-out.

Douglas's wife is appalled by the idea. Cash's girlfriend is scared.

The entire community gathers at a nearby bullfight arena dressed in their Sunday best. In a holiday mood, they pass the alcohol and place bets on the outcome of the altercation.

An announcer introduces Cash and Douglas as they stride to the center of the arena. The crowd becomes hushed. A bell tolls the hour—the signal to draw.

Shots ring out and Douglas falls to the ground. The camera pans the faces of the shocked crowd as they realize what they've done; they've wagered on a man's life.

The story concludes in a scene with Douglas's wife and son, the grief they suffer as they prepare for his funeral.

Aha! But that's not the end of the film.

There's a flashback, and this time we see Cash fall dead to the ground, followed by the faces of the shocked crowd. Saddened by her loss, his girlfriend prepares to leave town.

On the street she sees Douglas with his happy family. The two women lock eyes in mutual understanding.

Who really died? The audience makes the choice. It's an open ending.

Ending with a beginning

...to be continued. One story reaches a conclusion but is catapulted forward with a new hook that awaits a resolution in the next book, sequel, or movie.

> **Note to self...**
>
> *Choose with care how I resolve and conclude the story. My reader will remember the inspiration, fear, love, hate, passion and adventure forever.*

Speedy R & D – Research & Development

What we know...

Are you an attorney, biologist, gas station clerk or hairdresser? We can draw from what we know—our environment and our expertise. Our characters and descriptions will be more believable and their senses sharper when we write from our own knowledge. Not only will this add credibility, it also lends weight in a proposal to an agent or publisher. It becomes a part of your platform.

What we don't know...

Whether you want to camp by a stream to learn how your protagonist feels while he's fly fishing or ride the Indy track to see what your character observes, we have an open portal through the Internet. Yes, walk down the street with your people, sense the scent of orange blossoms in Southern California in January, and use libraries and museums to gather unique information. But sometimes you will need to take the internet shortcut to knowledge. Here is a list of resources available to us:

Internet Search Engines: Type in your subject—a word, name, place—and there it is, ready to be used in your story. Do you need a recipe? (There are seldom copyright restrictions on these.) Maybe you need the actual date of an event? The weather patterns in Southern Italy? Photos, dates, directions, and videos await the click of your Enter key.

Maps and Aerial Sites: Without traveling to France you have the ability to zoom in on a street with the Road Map choices. Choose Bird's Eye or 3D and you can see up-close terrain, places, streets, buildings. Try rotating the 3D and Bird's Eye features to see all sides of your subject. Trucks, lakes or cattle can be seen and described in your book. This will give you the ability to write plausible, detailed descriptions. (*www.bingmaps.com* and *www.earth.google.com*)

WebCam: These are similar to Map and Aerial, but are live. Try *www.earthcam.com* and see the exciting things that come up. You can choose from thousands of webcams.

Biographical profiles: It's easy to learn about people through these and they make great character studies. You'll be surprised to see who you can find out there. Type your name into your browser window. If you have any published quotes or works, achievements or school activities, they will come up for you and the world to view..www.wikipedia.com is another great source of information.

More Resources: Writing something about young children? Visit a kindergarten or day-care center. Is your protagonist a golfer? Go to the Pro-Shop. Put yourself out there and see what happens.

Contact a location in your story and make an appointment to go there. They may open doors you never imagined were possible, and there you are, taking notes and photos on the inside.

Jargon: Each walk of life and profession has its peculiar jargon. Is your scene set in the maternity ward of a hospital? Spy. Learn med-speak. Sit in the waiting areas, coffee shop or cafeteria and eavesdrop. Do you want to know more about the interior of a building that is otherwise off-limits? See if they offer a tour.

Today's savvy readers want to hear, feel, think, smell and see as the characters do.

They want to *be* the character and walk in his/her shoes.

> *'The most essential gift for a good writer is a built-in, shock-proof, shit detector.*
>
> Ernest Hemingway

Writer's Block

You have a great story idea, and either at the beginning, or deep into the heart of your plot, you run smack into a wall. Your brain flat-lines and you have nothing to write.

Questions come to haunt you: What makes me think I can write fiction? I'm not trained to do this, so why bother? What happens next to my characters? I'm running on empty.

Pages have been written about this plague—*writer's block*—the black hole of writing.

The major reasons for this might include:

- Lack of confidence and not being familiar enough with your subject and characters.
- Fear of people or the presures of a time line. What will readers think about my writing? My agent is expecting

this by next week. I have to get these edits done by tomorrow.

- Interruptions—your wife sticks her head in the door to your office and wants to know if you've seen the screwdriver anywhere. The buzzer on the dryer goes off and when you return from folding the clothes, your thread of thought has gone up in steam.
- You've come to the end of a scene and written a mini-resolution... now what? Where do my characters and the plot go from here? Your brain is vacant, empty, unavailable, expressionless, vacuous, unoccupied, barren, desolate, derelict and forsaken.

Is that how you feel? Then here are some block busters:

- Be alone.
- Turn off the telephones.
- Set aside a specific block of time to write when you are least likely to be disturbed by anyone, including the dog.
- Sit in a comfortable position, change chairs, add a pillow.
- Leave your writing space for a few minutes, do some stretches, take a short walk.
- Create absolute silence.
- Meditate and visualize. You see the big picture, now narrow it down to a simple scene.
- Keep a pad of paper and a pen next to your bed...when you wake up with an idea, don't think you'll remember it in the morning.
- Take a relaxing bath, a hot-tub break or a brisk swim.
- Set the scene for yourself. Listen to music that is conducive to the subject you are writing...romance, fast-paced thriller, horror, etc.
- Light candles and use aromatherapy to set the mood.

Some Good Exercises to Try

- Rehearse in your mind your outline (Through-Line). Then have your characters begin a conversation. Even if you never use the content of it they may lead you down a new and exciting road and help get your writing jump-started.
- Read the last few pages that you wrote to bring yourself up to speed.
- Close your eyes and envision what will happen next.
- Empty your mind of all thoughts. Don't think of what you need from the store, or when you have to pick up the kids. Empty your brain. Void. Meditate.
- Warm-up by writing a sentence or a line of dialogue. Let it come from your muse or your subconscious. You can delete it later, but this can jump-start you into a scene.
- Turn on a faucet, start an avalanche, let the words flow. Visualize these, or your own image. Imagine a package of dried alphabet soup pouring onto your desk.

> A book is the only place in which you can examine a fragile thought without breaking it, or explore an explosive idea without fear it will go off in your face... It is one of the few havens remaining where a man's mind can get both provocation and privacy."
>
> Edward P. Morgan

SEVEN:
Things You Need To Know About Editing & Revising

Elements of Editing

First Read – As You Go

One way to edit and rewrite is to read as you go. If you are interrupted and must leave your story for several hours or days, come back and read and edit what you previously wrote. This can be in its entirety or select the last few pages or paragraphs. By doing this, you are accomplishing your first edit, or first read.

Another good exercise is to return to your work and read it to yourself out loud. This will give you a fresh acoustic view of the changes needed and give you confidence in your writing.

Whenever you write with the antiquated media of pen (or pencil) and paper, and then transfer this into your computer, you are doing an edit. Likewise with a voice recorder.

Second Read – Content

When your novel is complete, put it away for no less than two weeks. Two months is better. Send your characters on a vacation and put the story out of your mind. Don't allow it to return until you are ready and can devote the time necessary to do a thorough read.

This time you go from page one to the end without stopping. A good way to do this is to print a copy (also supplying yourself with a hard-copy backup).

For this read, no pencils, pens or erasers are allowed. Even if it frustrates you not to make a correction, don't, because this read is for content. You'll have time the next go-through. At most, make a tick mark or underline a word or paragraph that needs changes.

Third Read – Revisions

This is where you can flesh out your characters, see how your dialogue resonates, fill in your scenes and setting.

Maybe you find a more suitable name for one of your people, or change someone's occupation. Revisions can go from a single word to entire paragraphs and chapters.

If your timeline is off, use your cut and paste features to take scenes to a new area of the book.

Revisions are slow and tedious, but try to look at it as filling in the blanks, or adding a few more clichés (just kidding), and taking time to smell the roses.

You need this experience to dwell with your characters on a very personal level. Sit down with one of them and have a conversation. Ask them if there is anything else they want to add in the story that will make them real in your readers mind. Get into each character's head, walk the walk, and build as you go.

An interesting exercise is to write down the number of words in your manuscript before you begin your revision. Some will say that revising will shorten your word count as you tighten the sentences, make your paragraphs succinct and defined. But the word count will also grow as you add more insight and depth to your people and their environment.

Fourth Read – Line or Copy Edit

Things like poor word choice, stiff dialogue, or awkward writing are corrected in this reading. Minor flaws that can usually be fixed with a word change or two are taken care of. Punctuation, spelling and grammar are corrected.

Peer through a magnifying glass at every word, sentence and nuance to weed out errors. Run it through Spell Check. Take each of the junk words in the list presented earlier in this book, and find ways to replace them.

Look at your margins, indents and the overall layout. When an agent or publisher sees your work for the first time, they expect—demand—that it be perfect. Gone are the days when you could submit 'a good story' and have the publisher ecstatic to the point of buying it on content alone, passing it on to their editors to solve your punctuation and grammar problems for you. Why? They don't have to. They receive too many submissions daily, solicited or not, that are print ready.

Okay, this is the time to grade your work. Here are the elements you need to check as you read, re-read, revise and line edit. Make a copy of this list and paste it on your forehead from the minute you write the first word to the last sentence of your novel. These are things that are essential in writing and editing fiction:

- Is your setting crisp, cinematic and full?
- Are your characters fleshed out, rounded, real? Believable?
- Does your dialogue carry the story?
- Do you take unnecessary time with narrative?
- Have you stayed in Point of View within each scene and chapter?
- Are there author intrusions? If so, eliminate them, or incorporate helpful ones smoothly.
- Do you catapult each scene and chapter ahead with a resolution and new hook?
- Have you thoroughly researched your subjects and places for accuracy?
- Are there disjointed actions or thoughts that will jolt your reader away from the story?
- Is your dialogue stilted or awkward? Try listening with care to everyday talk
- Does your story lag, include unnecessary phrases, or take the reader away from the plot? If so, do some tightening.
- Is the pace congruent with the action and plot?
- Do you avoid word repeats in close conjunction?
- Are your verbs active rather than passive?
- Do you avoid overuse of -ly words, adjectives, adverbs?
- Did you clip clichés?

Outside Read – Family, Friend, Editor?

At this point, you'll agree that writing is a lonely art. Friends and family will praise you for your efforts, but don't expect them to become involved. Yes, they'll ask to read it, but don't confuse that with *actually* reading it.

When To Let a Friend or Family Member Read Your Novel

Is this person a reader of the same genre and do you know them to be forthright and honest, or are they the type to praise for the sake of building your ego?

Most family members are reluctant to read what we have written. This may make no sense to you. On a personal note, when my daughter Hope read my *The Spaghetti Wars,* she summed up the problem:

> *"Mom, I love the story, the premise, the characters and the action. I get immersed in a scene and I'm involved with the series of events, happy to lose myself... when up pops the voice of my mother!"*

Do your friends/family know things about your subject/plot that can contribute to the overall story?

Stephen King, and many other prolific writers, have a set group of friends upon whom they can rely to read a story and offer sound critique. No flowering over, no placating—just the truth.

Writers develop the ability to accept criticism about their writing and the rejection of their submissions.

Hire a Professional Editor

Rates vary, but a good editor is worth the expense. You must choose the right person or company. Caution is advised, however. Some will claim to know the business, but still you should ask for references and credentials. Otherwise you're wasting time and money, and worse, you may take their advice and find out it's wrong, costing you the ultimate loss - publication and sales.

Join a Workshop or Critique Group

A good critique group can be invaluable. Many popular writers developed their writing skills while involved in a writing group. On the other hand, a bad group can ruin your writing. There are critique group horror stories of jealousy, ignorance, lack of tact, wrong information, callousness, and plain stupidity. This can't be allowed.

You will know a reputable group if they offer guidelines, have a facilitator versus a free-for-all 'read and bleed', and stick to the rules of critique etiquette. This is a great place to read your work out-loud or have a member read it. Don't forget, once the *'read and bleed'* session is over, you need not adhere to any advice that you received. It's your book.

Over-writing, Over-thinking, or How to Totally Screw Up a Good Novel

With today's economy, it would be expensive and cumbersome to print every version of our writing. We have the capability of saving files after each write, but it's tedious to go back and re-think the work.

Nevertheless, writers are inherently insecure. The more we receive rejections the greater our doubts.

Our first reaction is to *fix it*. Does someone order us to do this? Did you receive a lengthy critique, giving you the information needed to revise? Probably not.

We correct, over-correct, slash, kill, hack, chop, overthink, self-degrade, wear out erasers, wear the print off of the Backspace and Delete keys of our computers, over-develop, under-rate, over-describe, under-mine our work and shoot ourselves in the foot with or without clichés. Whether in first-person, God voice, or narrative, it makes no difference. You wrote it—therefore it is bad. A romance novel can be whittled down to this: *She said yes—he died.*

You killed it, baby.

Take heart. The first words we write on a subject, or from a characters mouth, are inspired by our muse. Is this muse infallible? No, so we do our best to correct the errors of their ways. Still, don't become obsessed with editing. Check the grammar, punctuation and leave it. Content edits will reveal places we need to change, but always maintain your creative spark.

Remember Tom Clancy's advice!

Keep at it. The one talent that's indispensable to a writer is persistence. You must write the book, else there is no book. It will not finish itself. Do not try to commit art.

Just tell the damned story.

Tools For Editing and Revising

A Short List of Editorial Must-Haves

- *The Elements of Editing – A Modern Guide for Editors and Journalists* - by Arthur Plotnik
- *Self-Editing for Fiction Writers* - by Renni Browne and Dave King
- *Revising Fiction – A Handbook for Writers* by David Madden
- *The Chicago Manual of Style – The Essential Guide for Writers, Editors, and Publishers* by The University of Chicago Press

A handy tool provided to us by Microsoft™ Word software is found beneath the *Review Tab* is *Tracking Changes* and *Showing Markups*. Apple™ Mac users will also find tracking capabilities. This can be confusing at first, but stay with it, it's of great use in editing your work, or others.

Once your submission is accepted by a publisher or editor you will likely work with them electronically using the tracking features.

How important is editing? Do you want to hang on to the idea that someone out there in the publishing world will be thrilled to edit your sure-to-be best-selling book? Probably not. Must you read and correct your work more than one time? Absolutely.

An editorial source claims that galleys (galleys are uncorrected proofs of your novel that your publisher sends to you) require two quality readings.

Maybe at this point in the process, 99% of the errors have been corrected. What about that remaining 1%? It could cost hundreds of dollars if one teensy little mistake is made, especially where figures are concerned.

Of course you will use your spell/language checker, dictionary and thesaurus. Read out-loud, put your manuscript to bed and reread it with fresh eyes—but DO NOT allow errors to remain in your work. It speaks for you in a positive or a negative way. It sets apart the amateur from the professional. (Now let's test the gimlet eye of my editor).

This is the final suggestion I can offer - hire a professional editor!

A Checklist of Reads and Edits

Who do you know and trust that you can turn your writing over to and feel confident that they will give you a thorough honest assessment?

First read...On The Go
Date:
Word Count:
Major Problems:
Second Read – Content:
Date:
Word Count:
Major Problems:
Third Read – Revisions:
Date:
Word Count:
Major Problems:
Fourth Read – Line or Copy Edit:
Date:
Word Count:
Major Problems:
Outside Read – Family, Friend, Editor?
Date:
Word Count:
Major Problems:

EIGHT:
Things You Need To Know About Publishers and Publishing

Preparing to Publish

Who to Submit a Manuscript to - an Agent or a Publisher?

Your manuscript is nearing completion and questions begin to arise regarding the multifaceted publishing world. The industry itself is fraught with change and uncertainty.

We see the major chain Barnes & Noble is busy, as well as corner stores who feature a specific genre; but others are struggling financially or going out of business altogether. Used bookstores thrive by giving credit for exchanging books, CDs and movies. Internet swap sites have grown during the past few years. One of these is *www. - paperbackswap.com.*

www.amazon.com is a world leader in book sales and distribution. Small community book readings are forming daily. Celebrities have started up book clubs.

Despite this growth pattern, we hear doubters claiming that the industry is failing.

No, the business of publishing books is morphing, or exploding, into fresh technology.

Instead of allowing these trends to bewilder us, we can declare ourselves to be twenty-first century publishing pioneers. Not long ago our choices to break into the world of published authors consisted of find an agent, find a publisher, or print and distribute the material on our own. In the 80's came the option to self-publish through small presses.

Today, internet e-commerce has revolutionized the author/publisher relationship. An aspiring author must first answer the following questions and choose which direction best suits his/her needs.

- Will a small publishing house work best with my fiction?
- Should I approach large publishing houses with my query, synopsis and manuscript?
- Will I be better served to sign with an agent?
- Do I want to self-publish?

The work involved, and the daunting amount of time required, can stop would-be self-published authors cold.

Some will point out that we must switch from the creative right side of our brain to the practical minded sales man dwelling in the left side. The good news is, you've begun this process while in the editing and layout stages of your fiction.

Next is an outline of the above four options, but I've omitted information on how to approach and solicit these until a later section.

Going to a Large Publishing House

Here's where the great success stories are realized—along with the tales of horror. Yes, they can promote your book in a big way. Their name alone will open doors and book shelves.

They have the power, the expertise and the funding. These are the people who offer mega-advances.

A word on advances... what does the name suggest to you? Yes, the money is an *advance against royalties* and you pay every penny back through future sales.

How can a first-time author get across the transom, and onto the desk of an editing clerk without diving head first into the slush pile?

The first words you'll read while perusing houses that print similar works to yours are—*We do not accept unsolicited manuscripts.* And—*We do not consider first-time authors.*

The only ways to get past this is to know someone inside the iron clad doors who will smuggle your work in and get it into the right hands, or you can sign with an agent.

The Shocking Truth...

Experts believe that the shelf life of a new book is less than 6 weeks. The clock begins ticking the second a book is placed on the shelf. If your book is selling, the bookstore may set up a standard monthly order. But if the store's computer discovers your book is sitting around gathering dust, off it goes to the distributor for credit.

The Small Publishing House.

For many years these were regional and selective. Press runs were large, thus the need for costly presses. Warehouses would fill with best-selling hardbacks and crates of paperback novels, at the houses expense.

In today's market we see *just-in-time* inventory. Because the distributors and the book store chains track inventory electronically, they order just what they estimate will be sold. Thus, a small house is affordable to operate.

With the advent of the small press, and the lower volume of printings per book, mom and pop publishing houses have multiplied nationwide, and they're hungry for authors and sales. Here you aren't likely to get lost in a maze of production processes and departments as you might in the large houses. You're apt to receive individual guidance and get to make more decisions about the layout and other options during the book-building process. The best reason? They are approachable. Just don't expect an advance check.

What You Can Expect From an Agent

Literary agents abound but don't expect to penetrate their fortresses without concise adherence to the criteria they set down for submitting.

- Agents know what editors and publishers are looking for and will narrow down the field, saving everybody time and expense.
- The material you submit to them must be perfect and exactly as they request.
- They will negotiate contracts with you and guide you through the publishing stages.
- Standard publishing contracts favor the publisher, not the author. An agent knows the ins and outs of these nuances.
- When an agent controls sub-rights, the author is likely to make more money.
- An agent wants to know that you can do your part in the editing, promotion and sales of your work. Remember, to publishers and agents you represent a commodity, so try not to take rejections personally. Your creativity creates their profits.
- They charge a percentage of the book sales, but if they are a member of the Association of Author's Representatives (AAR), they won't charge a reading fee.

Is having an agent worth the numbers involved? If you are a first-time author, want to get your book presented to large national publishers and would like to have an advocate who knows the ins and outs of the business, then yes.

In the *Complete Idiot's Guide, Getting Published - Fourth Edition,* Sheree Bykofsky and Jennifer Basye Sander team up as an agent and an editor to tell first-time authors that precisely because they both know the ins and outs of writing, they would never proceed as writers without having an agent to represent them. They indicated that having a good agent means you'll have less to worry about. In other words, even people in the publishing business use agents when they become authors.

Is Self-Publishing The Way to Go?

Ken Kesey, Virginia Wolfe, and Margaret Atwood self-published at one time or another. Dr. Wayne Dyer published *Your Erroneous Zones* and went on the road to sell it. He didn't quit until it became a world-wide best seller.

But will self-publishing gain you great acclaim? Probably not. What it does do is get what you've written in print for your own satisfaction, to sell or give away as you chose.

Now you'll need to switch from writing to running a business, from a perfect manuscript, to format, to production, purchasing, sales and revenue.

The big question becomes, what POD (Print on Demand)[1] press to choose, and what will that mean for you?

Print on Demand represents an efficient process that can be handled almost entirely electronically. Here are the issues surrounding POD:

[1] Print on demand is a computerized printing process that is used by almost all publishers—including the large commercial houses. It is being used here, however, to refer to publishers that charge an advance fee to have your book printed.

Set-up Costs

This is an either/or situation, because the printer will make his money whichever route you go.

If the POD charges zero set-up costs, they will charge more per book, pricing it out of the market, or pay lower royalties.

A higher set-up fee may translate to higher total profits later. If you don't expect to sell a high volume of your book, you will want to avoid set-up fees. When considering set-up costs, find out what they cover and don't pay for unnecessary services.

A basic package might include cover design, internal layout, an ISBN, and distribution to online retailers. Many packages add services that you can find at a lower price, such as copyediting, promotion, and copyright registration, which you can do yourself.

Cover Price

It costs more to print one copy of a book at a time, making cover prices for POD books higher than for mass market paperbacks. Up to $20 is the highest you can expect to receive for a soft-cover book. A POD publisher may charge over $22 for a 250 page book.

Other PODs, like *www.lulu.com*, will allow you to set your own cover price. Be sure this doesn't equate to a lower whole dollar per book royalty, but they do have a built-in calculator for you to experiment with.

A lower cover price may help you to sell more books, gaining what I call the *Walmart Effect.*

Royalties

POD publishers will pay you a percentage of net receipts. Others, like *Lulu.com* and *CafePress*, will let you set your own profit/royalty, which ultimately affects the cover price.

Royalties get convoluted too, because you don't get a solid idea of the actual money you'll receive. Plus the range of percentages offered makes it confusing when the distributors turn around and add a discount to retailers.

Some publishers assign different costs for printing the same size book.

Control

Do you want more artistic control over your book? Will you do your own design and layout?

Lulu.com would work for you if you want to have complete control of these things, including cover design. If not, they offer these services at a reasonable fee.

Or you may want to check out sites like *iUniverse*.

Do you want the ability to withdraw publication of your book for any reason, or to revise it? Having control allows you to seek a mainstream publisher for your book while it is being sold on demand and online.

Check out the contract terms to see what rights you are handing over to the publisher. Some PODs will demand exclusive rights to your work for a period of years.

Distribution

As we discussed earlier, most POD books will never see the inside of a brick and mortar store. If that is your goal, then you have to be certain that your POD will offer a reasonable discount to stores and accept returns.

You will want your book on Internet retail sites as well. Make sure your publisher plans to get your book listed on the mega-book websites. Don't keep it confined to just the one publisher's website.

Also, your POD will probably charge extra to drive your book to eBook readers.

Discounts

PODs generally offer an author volume discounts. If you're planning to buy copies for friends, local book store signings, or to donate to libraries, you will want this discounted price. But be sure that your discount is more than the royalty you would receive if the book were sold through your publisher's website.

POD Reputation

As in any venture, do your due diligence. Try typing *POD Publishers* into your browser and see what comes up. Some of these make statements that appear too good to be true.

If you come across a POD that offers low, or no set-up fees, and promises you your books will be stocked by the big chains, be careful. You can search out the PODs reputation with the BBB *(Better Business Bureau)* and in writer's forums on the Internet. Check reviews and compare through sites like *Publish on Demand* and *Books and Tales*.

Read carefully each publisher's website, and take a look at their contract, reading the fine print.

Finally, you can join the POD discussion list on Yahoo Groups. With a POD you have a tangible book of good quality, but there is a stigma that comes with it that hopefully will soon be gone.

You're on your own for marketing, and the book, and you, won't be given true publishing credits by most people in the industry.

The first question asked of an aspiring writer is, "*Are you published yet?*" If the answer is yes, the next question is, "*Who's your publisher, or did you self-publish?*"

Guess which answer gives you credibility.

The eBook

Do you want to publish electronically? Don't underestimate the value of this venue. There's more out there than the Sony Reader, Amazon Kindle, Nook, and iPad.

Strict validation requirements must be met in the process through *ePubCheck*. And you must present:

A copy perfect manuscript ready to upload.

- ✓ Choice of format such as pdf
- ✓ E-commerce capabilities such as PayPal, Visa, etc.
- ✓ Submit through an online e-book publisher: *Lulu.com, www.xlibris.com*, etc.
- ✓ Design everything on your own.
- ✓ Be ready to promote on your own.

Xlibris is owned by Random House, so they can be trusted to know the publishing business, in whatever form.

Some sources offer online classes and seminars. While another great resource is Joe Vitale's successful *www.7dayebook.com*. Find out if eBooks is the choice for you.

If you want to produce your own e.Book—and save money—there is a wonderful software product: Legend Maker (*www.LegendMakerStore.com*). Your manuscript is inserted along with tags to instruct the software where you want the chapter breaks, etc. The program goes to work and in a short time it produces your e-pub files, and saves them as an rtf file. Plus it is very affordable.

A final word on the above. These issues are changing so rapidly that by the time this book goes to press, the playing field and rules will have changed.

A book proposal from thought to transom takes a matter of hours. A full-length novel and the above list of satellite criteria, takes, on average, a minimum of one year. Two years is more realistic.

This is Your Query Letter Checklist

A proper letter format. No frills, no fancy paper, no gimmicks.

- ✓ An accurate name and address of the Agent/ Publisher!
- ✓ A brief introduction and description of the book.
- ✓ What is the target market for this book?
- ✓ A brief description of you, the author.

Of these, the last three are what take work. Lots of work.

Story Description

Start the drill-down by writing a two-paragraph description of your story.

Now use a pen, pencil or delete key to cross out every unnecessary word, adjective, adverb and repetition.

Once you've done this, condense your two paragraphs into two long sentences as succinct and with as much punch as possible.

You need to get the reader's attention within 50 to 100 words. Can you do that? Absolutely!

Here is a before and after example.

Without Sanctions

A 95,000 word thriller.

(1st draft)

Drexel Rose, a chess player, former Patriot's linebacker and a U.S. Surveillance Department expert, is one of an elite cadre of tactical stealth surveillance experts commissioned by U.S. President Miller to replace the NCS (National Clandestine Service).

A highly developed spy tank, ESD (Enemy Surveillance Department), can infiltrate satellite cloaking capabilities and cyber firewalls. Nothing, including political love-nests, can escape scrutiny. The ability to seek intelligence, without sanctions, has long been a controversial topic on Capitol Hill.

It is midnight Christmas Eve and a path of destruction begins in Boston, snaking down the eastern seaboard to the Kennedy Space Center. After the release of nuclear debris into the skies above Florida, a cyber virus is launched into the veins of NORAD's computer software leaving America vulnerable to attack by foreign enemies.

Most Federal employees are at home enjoying their holiday, and severe winter storms hammer most of the nation.

As is often the case, DHS, the CIA and the FBI start doing their typical who-does-what-now? ritual dance. It's Christmas and they have their fingers stuck in Figgy pudding.

Drexel and the members of ESD become drawn into this new game of home-grown idealist terrorism. They have fifty hours to stop the attacks that are advancing across the fifty states.

Drex is forced to go rogue if he wants to use the unsanctioned (Human) Brain-Computer Interface to get ahead of this new game being played on American soil.

This wouldn't even work on a jacket cover flap—plus it's too wordy.

So, let's try again.

(2nd draft)

Seeking intelligence without sanctions has long been a controversial topic on Capitol Hill. It's Christmas and Drexel Rose, a chess player, former Patriot's linebacker and a U.S. Surveillance Department expert must stop a group who are targeting America's most beloved icons.

Radioactive toxins have been released into the atmosphere and a lethal cyber-virus is transmitted into NORAD's software in Colorado. Drex is forced to go rogue if he wants to use the unsanctioned (Human) Brain-Computer Interface to get ahead of this new game being played on American soil.

This is chopped from 234 words to 85. Brutal—but not bad.

Target Market

The *Target Market* section can be developed in the same way. What author or book does this compare with? List who will want to read your story, why it will appeal to them, how it will reach a large audience, what the future potential is and credits or endorsements it has received:

Like Vince Flynn and Richard A. Clarke, action/thriller readers will choose Without Sanction *for its pace, wit and true life characters. As the first in a projected series of three, additional sales will generate with each release. The manuscript was a finalist in the Yosemite Writer's Conference fiction competition, and has been endorsed by the Assistant Director of the U.S. Secret Service (retired).*

The Author

Next is all about you. *A brief description of the author* is not as easy as it sounds. List your education, special studies, and accolades. Here is my attempt.

*I received my education in Boston and have studied under best-selling authors Sandi Ault (*Wild Indigo *and* Wild.Inferno, Berkley Prime Crime*), and Bonnie Hearn-Hill (*If It Bleeds, MIRA Books *and* Writer's Digest *contributor).*

Triad Press in Texas is featuring one of my short stories in a book to be released this year. I have founded and taught fiction writing classes and workshops in Texas, California, Colorado and Arizona..I'm presently working as an editor.......

The sequel, Without Limits, is underway and I believe both of these would be a great fit for you and your agency. I look forward to sharing this manuscript with you and thank you for your consideration.

Putting it all Together

Jan Holmes-Frost
1 Thorny Place
Tucson, AZ 85743

June 18, 20xx

Judy Van Agent
Van Agent Literary LLC.
New York, NY 10001

Dear Ms. Van Agent:

Seeking intelligence without sanctions has long been a controversial topic on Capitol Hill. It's Christmas and Drexel Rose, a chess player, former Patriot's linebacker and a U.S. Surveillance Department expert, must stop a group who are targeting America's most beloved icons. Radioactive toxins have been released into the atmosphere and a lethal cyber-virus is transmitted into NORAD's software in Colorado. Drex is forced to go rogue and use the unsanctioned (Human) Brain-Computer Interface to get ahead of this new game being played on American soil.

Readers of Vince Flynn and Richard A. Clarke's action/thrillers, will choose *Without Sanction* for its pace, wit and true to life characters. The manuscript was a finalist in the Yosemite Writer's Conference fiction competition, and has been endorsed by the Assistant Director of the U.S. Secret Service (retired).

I received my education in Boston and studied under best-selling authors Sandi Ault (*Berkley Prime Crime*), and Bonnie Hearn-Hill (*MIRA Books* and *Writer's Digest* contributor). Triad Press in Texas is featuring one of my short stories in a book to be released this year. I teach fiction writing classes and workshops in Texas and Arizona, and am currently employed as an editor.

The sequel, *Without Limits,* is underway and I believe the projected series of three to be a good fit for your agency. I look forward to sharing this manuscript with you and thank you for your consideration.

Sincerely,

Of the above list of twelve tools for seeking publication, the query letter is the only one to be detailed in this book. The rest are self-explanatory or instructions can easily be found. Now that you have your list filled, what next?

It's time to find those agents and publishers. There are many trackers available, but one of the best for including everything needed is *www.querytracker.net*. Here you'll find access to agents listed by genre allowing you to peruse those who are seeking similar works to your own.

From there you can click on each agent's website and find their submissions guidelines. Do not vary from what they ask. Today's agents do accept electronic submissions, but usually the query will be in the body of your email.

Don't attach or send anything other than what they want. The letters on their Delete key are worn off for good reason.

Writing is a lonely art, so get involved in your local writing community for support and inspiration. Find your voice, give it a vehicle and listen to your muse as you journey to success!

> To finish is a sadness to a writer—a little death. He puts the last word down and it is done. But it isn't really done. The story goes on and leaves the writer behind, for no story is ever done.
>
> John Steinbeck

For the Finest in Nautical and Historical Fiction and Nonfiction

WWW.FIRESHIPPRESS.COM

Interesting • Informative • Authoritative

All Fireship Press and Cortero Publishing books are available directly through www.FireshipPress.com, Amazon.com and via leading wholesalers and bookstores throughout the U.S., Canada, Europe, and soon Australia.

E